CESSNA
CITATION JETS

Geza Szurovy

MBI Publishing Company

First published in 1999 by MBI Publishing Company, 729 Prospect Avenue, PO Box 1, Osceola, WI 54020-0001 USA.

MBI Publishing Company books are also available at discounts in bulk quantity for industrial or sales-promotional use. For details write to Special Sales Manager at Motorbooks International Wholesalers & Distributors, 729 Prospect Avenue, PO Box 1, Osceola, WI 54020-0001 USA.

Library of Congress Cataloging-in-Publication Data available

ISBN 0-7603-0785-7

On the front cover
Cessna flagship is the world's fastest business jet, the Mach .90 plus Citation X. Announced at the 1990 NBAA convention, the airplane is a brand new, "clean sheet" design rather than a derivative. The $17 million, 8-10 passenger Citation X is at the upper end of the mid-sized range of business jets, yet its performance figures put it more in league with larger jets.

On the frontispiece
Welcome aboard! With a side-hinged door and integral boarding ladder, the CitationJet's self-contained entry way is similar to the doors of other Citations.

On the title page
Note the flap drive seals on the trailing edge to keep drag at bay and make the CitationJet a 380-knot airplane.

On the back cover
The Sovereign is intended to be a true transcontinental workhorse with a 2,500- nautical mile NBAA IFR range carrying eight passengers at 400 knots. On shorter distances it can cruise at speeds up to 445 knots. Its maximum certified altitude is 47,000 feet.

The photos on the following pages are courtesy of Quadrant Picture House: 23, 24, 29 (bottom), 39, 40 (top), 42 & 43.

Edited by Mike Haenggi
Designed by Todd Sauers
Printed in China

Contents

Introduction

Cessna's Citations are without a doubt the most successful executive jets in terms of the sheer numbers flying compared to the rest of the fleet. Since the late 1970s, Cessna has continuously held approximately half of the light to medium business jet market.

From humble beginnings, zeroing in on the entry-level light jet market segment ignored by the other business jet makers, Cessna now has the broadest product line ranging from the light CJ1 to the world's fastest business jet, the Mach .92 super-mid-sized Citation X.

In the last 30 years Cessna has sold over 3,000 Citations and has been twice awarded the prestigious Collier Trophy for its efforts with the Citation line. Such results are the fruit of consistently having been the most customer-sensitive business jet maker in the industry, always listening, always striving to deliver what its potential customer base requests.

But Cessna hasn't just listened. It has also inspired its customers to demand such leading-edge jets as the CitationJet and the X. Both push the envelope in their own way, and both came into being because Cessna guaranteed its trusting customers that they could be done, and then delivered. The turn of the millennium is a fine time to pause and look back on the Citations to better follow their adventures to come in the 21st century.

Several people have been helpful in making this book possible. I would particularly like to thank Jennifer Whitlow, Ed Parrish, Jan MacIntyre, and all the photographers who've been bringing us the spirit of the Citations over the years.

1

Chapter One

Revolution

A gray, ragged ceiling hung low over Wichita's Municipal Airport on the morning of September 15, 1969. The murky sky was frustrating the efforts of a small group of engineers, test pilots, ground support staff, and executives from Cessna Aircraft to launch the company's latest prototype on its maiden flight by its scheduled 9:15 A.M. takeoff time.

The first marketing teaser of the shape of things to come from Cessna. Few remember that the company had already joined the jet age in the 1950s with its T-37 military trainers.

The Fanjet mock-up held true to the artist's impression, but the prototype had even more pleasing lines.

The airplane they were preparing for its moment of truth was like no other Cessna before it. It was the Citation, a captivating little executive jet and the biggest gamble in the long and distinguished history of a company renown for its piston-powered aircraft line ranging from the Cessna 150 two-seat trainer to the Cessna 421 Golden Eagle pressurized cabin class twin. If the Citation succeeded, it would propel the company into the new and potentially lucrative jet league. If it failed, Cessna, the world's dominant piston airplane manufacturer, would be increasingly hard pressed to find other opportunities for growth.

By mid-afternoon the weather was beginning to cooperate and final preparations for the Citation's maiden flight were completed. Test pilots Milt Sills and Jim LeSueur climbed on board and began to methodically work their way through their checklists. With everything proceeding normally, they fired up the two Pratt & Whitney JT15D-1 engines as they had so many times before for the low- and high-speed taxi tests. But this time they were taxiing out to fly.

At 3:20 P.M. the Citation accelerated down the runway with Milt Sills in command. Seconds later it reached rotation speed and Sills smoothly lifted it into the air. They had used barely 1,500 feet of the runway to get airborne.

Sills and LeSueur were scheduled for a 45-minute test flight, but everything went so smoothly that they extended the sortie by an hour. They cycled the gear, performed a variety of handling and systems checks and accelerated the Citation up to

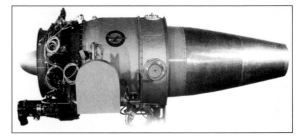

Displayed with the mockup, which was introduced at the 1969 NBAA convention, is the Pratt & Whitney JT15D that made the Citation possible. Key to its success was that it was a fanjet, much more economical to run than the low-bypass jets used on most other business aircraft at the time.

Days before its first flight, the Fanjet became the Citation. Borrowed from the famous Triple Crown winner, the name was devised by business jet marketing guru Jim Taylor to differentiate Cessna's new jet from the names of its competitors. The plane's maiden flight went perfectly and it went on to change business aviation.

225 knots. The pesky ceiling restricted them to an altitude of 10,000 feet instead of the planned climb to 20,000 feet, but the test flight was a total success, topped off with a perfect touchdown.

From such auspicious beginnings the Citation went on to become the best-selling executive jet in the world. Over 3,000 Citations of all types were sold by the turn of the century, and the current product line features eight models, ranging from the entry-level CitationJet to the world's fastest business jet, the Citation X.

As is often the case with an exceptionally successful business venture, the Citation was a runaway initial success because its creators saw an opportunity overlooked and even disdainfully dismissed by its competitors. It has maintained its winning streak because Cessna has proven to be as adept at continuing to discern and deliver exactly what the market wants as it was at identifying the initial opportunity.

The beginnings of the concept that would lead to the Citation can be traced back to the mid-1960s. The jet age had dawned on the airliners barely a decade before and commercial passenger jets still held many people in awe as an exotic leading-edge technological accomplishment. Even more exotic was the rarefied world of a handful of business jets that had arrived on the scene. Most were the products of companies experienced in military or commercial jet production with price tags to match, such as the North American Saberliner, the four-engined Lockheed Jetstar, the British Hawker Siddeley HS 125, and the French Dassault Falcon 20.

It took a maverick outsider who had never designed an airplane in his life to realize that there was room for a small, less expensive executive jet to provide jet airliner performance at a price that companies could afford and were willing to pay. His name was Bill Lear, and his masterpiece, the Learjet, became a synonym for executive jet for decades to come. Going head to head with the Learjet was Aero Commander's less glamorous but equally capable Jet Commander 1121 designed by Ted Smith.

The three core makers of general aviation airplanes, Piper, Beechcraft, and Cessna, had to decide how to respond to the jet age. The challenge they

Celebrations after the first flight. Test pilot Milt Sills is on the left, next to him is Dwane Wallace, Cessna's Chairman and CEO. Test pilot Jim LeSueur is to the right of the data probe. Like its namesake, the Triple Crown winner, the Citation wears a winner's wreath.

faced was figuring out how to ramp up their design and technological capabilities from what it took to make the light piston airplanes that accounted for the bulk of their production to the standards demanded by the more complex jets. Given the capital required to get into the startup general aviation jet game, none of the players could afford an error in judgment.

The three companies chose different paths that ultimately allowed Cessna to grasp its opportunity. Piper decided to do nothing. Beechcraft entered the jet age by going the turboprop route. Olive Ann Beech's company redesigned the piston Queen Air around the newly available compact Pratt & Whitney Canada PT6 turboprop engine and called it the King Air. Beechcraft thus created the most successful general aviation turboprop of the century that is still going strong at the end of the millennium.

Beechcraft also entered into an agreement to market the Hawker Siddeley HS 125 in the United States, a graceful way around the need to commit mountains of capital to develop a clean sheet business jet in-house. Later Beechcraft would rely on acquisition to establish its own line of jets. In 1986 the company bought the Mitsubishi Diamond II production line and developed it into the Beechjet. Ironically, in 1992, long after the Hawker marketing agreement was history, Beechcraft also acquired the Hawker production line from British Aerospace, the company into which Hawker Siddeley had been by then folded by the British government.

Cessna tread cautiously in these potentially treacherous waters, initially opting to view developments from the sidelines. At the time Cessna's piston airplanes accounted for half the 100,000 airplanes that made up the general aviation fleet and the company was merrily cranking out well over 10,000 airplanes a year. But it could see a fair share of its top-of-the-line twin customers flocking to Beechcraft's friendly King Air that delivered jet technology and turboprop performance easily manageable by pilots with only piston twin experience.

Further up the general aviation product line Cessna saw the Learjet, the Jet Commander and the heavier iron beyond them, all competing feverishly to provide jet airliner performance, and demanding jet airline pilot skills from their crews. Swept-wing

From the beginning the Citation had outstanding visibility. Ease of operation and safety were top priorities for the company.

aerodynamics and flight management aids were much less advanced back then, making the early jets much less forgiving of any pilot imprecision. The business jets were hot ships even for turboprop pilots, let alone for pilots planning to step up into the big time from piston equipment.

Yet the business jet makers weren't focused on making life easier for pilots transitioning up into their airplanes. Their sights were set on flying higher, faster, and farther. Only pilots with the right stuff need apply. The gap between the business jets and turboprops was vast. And therein Cessna saw an opportunity.

Why not build a six-seat business jet that would be as easy to fly as a King Air, yet cruise about 100 knots faster, get in and out of the same small airfields, fly as high as 35,000 feet, and be almost as economical to buy and operate. It wouldn't be as fast as a Learjet, but it would cost considerably less and a pilot wouldn't need Chuck Yeager's genes to fly it well. Business jet aficionados may have scoffed at the idea of "building down," but Cessna's strategic thinkers saw a lot of aspiring jet pilots jumping at the chance to fly just such an airplane.

To attain the desired benign handling characteristics and low-approach speeds, it would be a straight-wing design. To be economical, it would have to be powered by a turbofan engine that consumed about 30 percent less fuel than the turbojets that powered the other business jets. Simple systems would also help keep costs in check. The jet would be easy enough to fly to allow single pilot operation, just like the King Air and the piston twins.

Finding a suitable engine would be a challenge. While turbofans were already in existence, one small enough to suit Cessna's purpose was yet to be developed.

The more Cessna contemplated such an entry-level business jet, the more promising it looked. In spite of being best known for its mass-produced 150s and Skyhawks, Cessna already had much of the experience in-house to build the jet. Its top-of-the-line twin was the cabin class Cessna 421 Golden Eagle. It was pressurized, able to maintain an 8,000 foot cabin at 20,000 feet, and the technology used to build its airframe was in many ways similar to what would be required to build the proposed jet.

But Cessna had another ace up its sleeve, one that is often forgotten. It was already an experienced jet airplane manufacturer. It had designed and since 1957 was delivering to the Air Force the T-37B primary trainer. The Tweety Bird, as it was affectionately known, was a side-by-side two-seat jet trainer powered by two GE J-69 engines licensed and built by Continental that delivered 1,025 pounds of static thrust each. It had a maximum speed of 375 knots and a service ceiling of 35,100 feet. Shortly after getting its first batch of Tweety Birds, the Air Force switched to *ab initio* jet training for its pilots.

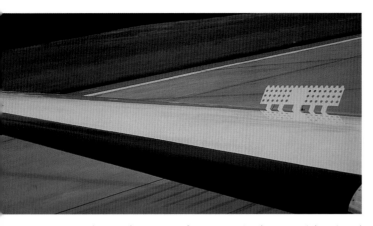

The spoilers are a feature retained on straight-winged Citations since the first prototype.

By 1968 the 1,000th T-37 was delivered to the Air Force and Cessna began producing a ground attack version of the airplane. This was the A-37B Dragonfly, equipped with more powerful GE J-85 engines that produced 2,850 pounds of thrust each. The A-37B had a combat gross weight of 14,000 pounds of which 5,680 pounds could be external ordnance consisting of napalm, rockets, and a minigun. Its top speed was 456 miles per hour and its service ceiling was 41,765 feet. Whatever experience Cessna may have lacked with its domestic programs to build the contemplated executive jet, it amply made up for on the military side.

By 1967 Cessna's Chairman, Dwane Wallace, was convinced that the proposed executive jet made good business sense. Dwane, an aeronautical engineer, and his brother, Dwight, a lawyer, were nephews of Clyde Cessna, founder of the firm. They had learned to fly on their uncle's lap when they were kids, and in 1934 they resurrected the company after it closed its doors during the Great Depression. Back then they had let it be known that Cessna was back with Dwane's own design, the Airmaster, which to this day is one of the sleekest, fastest general aviation four seaters in spite of having become a valued antique.

Now, Dwane Wallace and his colleagues sensed another opportunity for a landmark step forward and committed Cessna to joining the jet set.

By the fall of 1968 the design had progressed far enough to make its public debut. On October 7, at the National Business Aircraft Association (NBAA) convention in Houston, Texas, Cessna announced the launch of what it tentatively designated the Fanjet 500 (naming it the Citation was yet to come). The 500 designation was the company's next model number after its 400-series cabin class piston twins.

The mock-up at the NBAA convention presented a good broad-brush idea of the jet's likely appearance, but as the design was finalized and refined in wind tunnel tests its lines gradually evolved into what has since become the classic Citation look.

A key event that allowed the project to proceed was the identification of a suitable engine that was already under development. Seeking to leverage its successful PT6 turboprop engine, Pratt & Whitney Canada was developing its core design into a small turbofan, the 2,200-pound thrust JT15D. The Fanjet 500 would be the perfect launch airplane for the new engine. By the time the Fanjet 500 was announced at the NBAA convention, the JT15D was being test flown with promising results.

Work on the airplane was also progressing smoothly. Design simplicity was paramount. The fuselage was circular in cross section, the simplest shape to pressurize. It had room for six in the cabin, four in a club seating arrangement, and two in adjoining seats.

The straight wing was no more complex than the wings of cabin class piston twins and the King Air. It had a fail-safe design. Its spar was made up of two elements joined together, either of which could carry the airplane's full load alone.

Mechanical linkages consisting of pushrods, pulleys, and cables operated the controls. Simple, electrically driven flaps slowed the jet to pattern and approach speeds more in line with piston aircraft.

The main gear had a wide wheelbase for comfortable ground handling and retracted into the wings. The wheels rested snugly in the wheel wells, remaining exposed. They were flush with the wing's underside, requiring main gear doors only for the struts. The nose wheel was mechanically steerable through the rudder pedals, just like a Skyhawk.

Fuel was carried in two wing tanks each feeding the engine on its side. A simple crossfeed provided each engine access to fuel from the tank on the other side if required.

Wing and empennage de-icing was provided by pneumatic rubber boots, except for a small inboard portion of each wing which was de-iced with a heated metal edge that melted the ice and prevented large chunks from being thrown back by the slipstream into the engine intakes. The inboard panel de-icing came on automatically when the pilot selected engine intake de-icing.

While the prototype development was progressing well, Cessna faced one problem that went beyond design and engineering. It had to figure out how to sell its new jet. The successful marketing and sales of the piston line through a network of Cessna dealerships held by Fixed Base Operators (FBOs) was not an ideal formula for selling expensive executive jets. Relying on dealers would have made it difficult for the company to retain the close control over marketing and sales required to effectively develop relationships with sales leads for such a high ticket item. There was the additional challenge of having to introduce a radically new airplane on which a skeptical jury was still out.

Lacking the resources in-house, Cessna tackled its marketing problem by convincing the best man for the job to join the company. His name was Jim Taylor and he had just spent the last five years in charge of marketing at Pan American's business jet division, where his primary task was developing the market for the Falcon 20, for which Pan Am held the U.S. agency. Taylor started with one prototype demonstrator and by the time he left he had sold 125 Falcon 20s. This was an outstanding achievement for an unknown non-U.S. jet in the American market.

Taylor believed that a business jet was no different than any other large ticket item such as computer equipment, heavy machinery, or, for that matter, airliners. It should therefore be sold the same way, directly by company sales representatives working through a network of company-run regional sales offices, all under the umbrella of Cessna's newly established commercial jet marketing division.

Detail of the de-icing boot and the electrically heated wing root deicer that comes on automatically with the engine cowl de-icing system to prevent chunks of ice being ingested into the engine.

Another cornerstone of Taylor's marketing strategy was to sell a total package. The jets would be offered with a choice of avionics packages rather than an individually specified mix of avionics per airplane. They would be serviced at company-owned and-run regional service centers, and their pilots would be trained in a standardized training program contracted out to the training arm of American Airlines.

These measures achieved two objectives. They cut costs for Cessna that could be passed on to the customers, and they enabled the company to develop ongoing long-term relationships with their customers. This relationship nurturing proved crucially important to Cessna's success in later years. It generated a fierce customer loyalty that provided a captive pool of buyers over the coming decades.

One of Jim Taylor's first priorities after joining Cessna was choosing a more suitable name than Fanjet 500 for the new airplane he was about to sell. Fanjet just didn't have that inspiring spark Taylor was looking for, and it was too close to the competition's jet-minded monikers, such as Learjet and Jet Commander. Great effort was spent to look for a new name, involving Taylor, other senior executives, and even highly paid name consultants, but nothing any of them came up with took hold.

What Taylor wanted most was a name that conveyed a winner. His line of reasoning turned his thoughts to winning racehorses. And then he had it. Citation—the legendary winner of the Triple Crown. All that remained now was to convince Dwane Wallace and the rest of senior management to agree. But the last thing these conservative captains of the general aviation industry were inclined to do was name their new jet after a horse.

Undeterred, Taylor bought horseshoes. He had them silverplated and one morning he placed one on each of his colleagues' desks before they arrived for work. That did the trick. Ten days before its maiden flight, the Fanjet became the Citation. Like its namesake, it would prove to be a spectacular winner. And to this day the horseshoe forms part of the Citation logo.

On September 10, 1971 Dwane Wallace (right) is awarded the Citation 500's certificate of airworthiness by the FAA's regional representive.

Years before the Citation was planned, Cessna built jet experience with the T-37 trainer

A beautiful portrait of a Citation I, the first of many upgrades to the original 500.

Following its maiden flight, the Citation underwent an intensive two-year flight test and certification program that confirmed its projected performance. Cessna's 6/7 passenger executive jet could fly as far as 900 statute miles, cruise at 320 knots, climb as high as 35,000 feet, and use all the airports available to its turboprop competition. Its acquisi-tion and operating costs, while somewhat higher than a turboprop, were well below the costs of other executive jets. And above all, it was one of the best handling, safest airplanes in general aviation.

The Citation was certified in the air transport category under FAR 25 to meet the same rigorous standards demanded of the airlines and reassure potential buyers with safety concerns. On September 10, 1971, the Citation received its FAA certification. The first production Citation went to American Airlines' Citation training facility and in early 1972

Milt Sills at the Citation X's controls a quarter century after taking the first ever Citation on its maiden flight. He could never have guessed back then where that first flight would lead.

SPECIAL MISSIONS

Cessna's T-37 Tweety Birds and A-37 Dragonflies weren't the only jets made by Cessna to serve the U.S. national interest. Several Citations also played roles at various times over the years. In 1984 15 Citation S/IIs joined the Navy, to take turns masquerading as an aggressor, no less. The Navy awarded Cessna a contract to modify 15 S/IIs to serve as training aircraft for undergraduate radar intercept operators (RIOs).

Specially modified executive jets are an exceptionally cost-effective way to train RIOs. They cost less to operate than purpose-built combat training aircraft, they are highly maneuverable, and can carry several aspiring RIOs and their instructor on a sortie. Designated T-47As, the Citations replaced the Navy's aging North American T-39Ds, which were modified Saberliners fulfilling the RIO training role.

The T-47As flew in pairs on a typical training sortie. One acted as a bogie (the bad guy) and the other set out to nail it, vectored into position by the trainee RIO, carefully watched by the instructor.

The mission's special demands required some modification in addition to installing the training electronics. To meet the Navy's maneuverability requirements, the S/II's wing span was reduced by five feet and the ailerons were hydraulically boosted, increasing the airplane's roll rate. For more power, the engines were upgraded to the JT15D-5, which delivered 2,900 pounds of thrust each, an increase of 400 pounds per side. This was the engine used four years later on the Citation V.

To withstand bird strikes when maneuvering at low level at 350 knots, the windshield was strengthened.

Civilian jets are restricted by the regulations to 250 knots below 10,000 feet, allowing the use of a weaker windshield to provide the same level of bird strike protection on the original Citation II. The T-47s also have a small window at the top of the cockpit to enable their crews to better keep an eye on each other during their VFR gyrations.

Under the contract, Cessna also provided the pilots (subcontracted to Northrop), maintenance, and the Singer-Link radar simulators.

Citation IIs are also used by the Drug Enforcement Administration for surveillance work along vulnerable borders. Airborne surveillance equipment lets the Citations track suspected drug smugglers in the air, on land, and in water, and coordinate their interception. In the Coast Guard, Citation IIs are used in search and rescue work.

And 12 years after the Citation S/II was selected by the Navy, Cessna got the opportunity to add the Army to its growing list of Citation clients, though in a more traditional role. In 1996 the Army chose the Citation Ultra for its Medium Range Transport to ferry VIPs around.

Levitz Furniture became the first customer to take delivery of a Citation for corporate use.

By the end of 1972 Cessna had delivered 52 Citations, making the airplane the best-selling business jet in its first year of production. As the sales figures would demonstrate in coming years, the Citation's impact on business aviation was revolutionary, making executive jets available to a vast, hitherto untapped market. Just how big a gamble Cessna had taken with the Citation is told by the company's financial figures. The $35 million Cessna had spent on developing the Citation amounted to 40 percent of its 1971 net worth.

Chapter Two

Evolution

The annual delivery figures for the four years after the first Citation 500 entered corporate transport service reveal what a homerun Cessna had hit by betting 40 percent of its net worth on its new jet. In 1972 the company delivered 51 Citations, followed by 80 in 1973, 84 in 1974, and 76 in 1975, more than any other maker of executive jets.

Note the TKS anti-icing system along the S/II's wing. It was infused with pinholes through which glycol "wept" onto the leading edge to prevent ice from forming.

This classic portrait reveals the Citation II's clean aerodynamic lines. Cessna would push the model line beyond belief in coming years through aerodynamic changes and engine upgrades. Speed would rise well beyond 400 knots and the cabin would grow to carry eight passengers. The II became so popular that it continued evolving well into the future as the Bravo.

crept up by 12 knots to 352 knots. Breaking the 350-knots barrier was a small but important psychological step toward dealing with the airplane's reputation for being slow. Range also improved, rising under the hypothetical standard conditions from 825 nautical miles to 942 nautical miles with IFR reserves. The original Citation 500s were upgradable to the more efficient engines and most were so modified.

The Citations' superb cockpit visibility is seen here on final approach to Raleigh Durham, North Carolina, in one of four Ultras operated by Lowe's Home Improvement Warehouse of North Wilkesboro, North Carolina.

Good baggage capacity is a Citation hallmark. The entire line is so well designed that it is practically impossible to inadvertently exceed weight balance limitations due to loading configuration on any Citation model.

This Citation II, seen at the 1999 Paris Air Show, soldiers on for Holland's Delft University of Technology as an airborne research platform. It is also a nice way to travel.

Also achieved in 1977 was the certification of the Citation I for single pilot operation, a milestone Cessna had craved since launching the original Citation. The model designation was Citation I/SP. It required minor modifications to the airplane, primarily the relocation of a few switches for easier single pilot access. Most of the change was a paperwork exercise, because the I/SP had to be certified under FAR 23 to qualify for being flown by a single pilot while the standard Citation I was certified under the more stringent FAR 25 that also applies to airliners.

The Citation I continued to be called the C-500 and remained the world's most popular entry-level business jet. By the time it went out of production in 1985 the number produced had risen to 342, pushing the grand total for all C-500s to 691.

The Citation I was eventually forced out of production by the increased prices Cessna had to pay for its engines. By the 1980s Pratt & Whitney upped the prices of the JT15D-1As to the point where the price difference between them and more powerful versions powering the bigger Citation II had become minimal. This forced Cessna to charge for the Citation I crept too close to the price of the Citation

II to remain competitive. The Citation I's demise, however, spurred Cessna to develop a modern replacement, the highly successful CitationJet.

In 1978, a year after the Citation I went into service, Cessna completed the first major upscaled derivative of the airplane, the Citation II. Much in the manner of airliner upgrades, the Citation II was basically a stretched I with more powerful engines and a beefed up, higher aspect ratio wing.

A 3.5-foot fuselage stretch made the Citation II an eight-seat airplane, excluding the pilots. The spar transitioned through the fuselage under the last row of seats, so the central cabin aisle remained unobstructed until the step up to the platform on which the aft seats were installed. Cessna also managed to extract another five inches of headroom over the aisle by adjusting the cabin's interior design.

To handle its larger load the Citation II was given more powerful engines, more fuel, and a wider wing span. Its Pratt & Whitney JT15D-4 engines could each belt out 2,500 pounds of thrust, 300 pounds more per engine than the Citation I. Fuel capacity was increased from 544 gallons to 742 gallons, and wing span expanded by 5.1 feet to

The little Citations soon took their place at the nation' airports, making life easier and more productive for their owners. The United 737 has access to 500 U.S. airports. The Citation can use 5,000.

A good view of the Citation S/II's wing shape. Compared to the Citation II, it is a much improved wing that pushed the Citation beyond 400 knots for the first time. The S/II's airfoil was completely different from the standard IIs, and it also featured swept-wing roots.

The nice thing about Citations is that they are equally at home at JFK and your friendly local airstrip. Here a Citation II shares the ramp with an experimental Europa on a Sunday morning.

improve performance and accommodate the extra fuel. All this upscaling meant extra weight, and the Citation II's maximum take-off weight worked out to 13,300 pounds.

The Citation II's performance represented significant progress over the Citation I. Its improved thrust-to-weight ratio enabled its more powerful engines to propel it along at 385 knots in normal cruise, still about 80 knots shy of a Learjet 35 but a big advance for the Citation. Its IFR range was a respectable 1,159 nautical miles and it was certified to 43,000 feet. It topped off its increased capabilities over the Citation I by retaining the lovely Citation handling characteristics and short field performance, and it was also certified for single pilot operation.

The Citation II continued to provide an alternative to the turboprops, which by then were beginning to chip away at the Citation I's speed advantage, yet it also gave serious competition to other light jets. On the short stage lengths of the typical corporate flight (the straight average is approximately 300 nautical miles), the Citation II was giving up only a few minutes of travel time to the opposition. For many buyers its ease of handling, simplicity, and lower price outweighed what they considered a relatively minor speed disadvantage.

The Citation IIs were literally flying out the company's hangar doors. They quickly became not only the best-selling Citation, but also the best-selling business jet overall. By 1982 when Cessna delivered the 1,000th Citation, a Citation II to Iridium Corporation of America headquartered in Utica, New York, Citations held 55 percent of the light jet market.

Nevertheless, the speed issue continued to irk the company. The Citation II was within 15 knots of the tantalizing 400-knots threshold. The marketing solution was to talk in miles per hour instead of knots, which instantly drove the normal cruise figure up to the much more impressive value of 426. But the engineers knew the truth and in the early

The Citation S/II was the first jet used by Executive Jet to establish the first fractional ownership program. From these beginnings the NetJets program went on to build a fleet numbering in the hundreds.

A fine por
one-piece
sure turbin

1980s they decided to do something about it. They would re-equip the Citation II with a new, high-speed wing.

The re-winged Citation II made its debut in 1984 and was designated the S/II (the S stood for Super, it is said). High-tech computer-aided design technology was employed to design the new wing's supercritical airfoil over the Citation II wing's plan form and basic structure. It had a leading-edge cuff and a flatter shape optimized for high-speed cruise. A swept-wing root, aileron and flap gap seals, and redesigned fuselage and engine nacelle fairings contributed to the war on drag. The

ailerons were made of graphite to keep weight under control.

Another major change was the wing and horizontal stabilizer de-icing system. Instead of the bulky boots, the S/II got a low drag "weeping wing" system that pumps ethylene glycol de-icing fluid through the tiny pinholes of a smooth metal leading edge. Technically it is an anti-icing rather than a de-icing system because the fluid prevents ice from forming, rather than melting formed ice.

It is the same system used on contemporary Hawkers and some light aircraft. It is effective but its drawbacks are a finite supply of heavy de-icing

31

Air travel in Ultra comfort. Cessna put extra effort into making the Ultra's cabin as luxurious as any on the executive jet scene. Careful recontouring of the interior increased headroom without any change in exterior dimensions.

In 1986, as Citation sales were approaching 1,500, the company received one of the highest honors in the aviation industry when it won the prestigious Collier Trophy for its line of business jets. Awarded to the Citation and Russ Meyer, who had succeeded Dwane Wallace at Cessna's helm in 1975, the commendation specifically cited the Citation's excellent safety record.

The drag reduction results of the S/II program told Cessna that there was still room left in the Citation to grow into something more capable. The company faced a strategic decision. Could it push the S/II enough to create sufficient product differentiation between it and the airplanes to justify making both of them? Is that what the market wanted? There seemed to be a substantial market segment

The
bo

A g
pne

The Ultra's modern, third-generation, integrated Honeywell glass cockpit. This was the first Citation with a full glass cockpit featuring integrated primary flight displays and multifunction displays.

This close-up of an Ultra shows the care taken with fairing in the swept-wing roots that originated on the S/II high-speed wing. The swept-wing roots significantly reduce drag at the wing fuselage juncture, allowing the jet's top speed to reach 430 knots.

whose needs and budget hankered for the original Citation II, and one that wanted more airplane and was willing to foot the bill. In the end Cessna decided to take the S/II to its limits as the Citation V and put back in production the popular Citation II.

It was clear from the S/II's aerodynamic cleanup that with more power the airframe was ready to race. There also was room to stretch the cabin without unduly sacrificing performance, so the Citation V was stretched by another 1.5 feet. This made the airplane comfortable for eight passengers in a double club seating layout with room for an aft lavatory.

The power upgrade that made this version of the Citation possible was the Pratt & Whitney JT15D-5A engine. It pumped out 2,900 pounds

of thrust, increasing total thrust available for the airplane by a massive 800 pounds. This put the Citation V's cruise speed reliably into the 415-425 knots range. It was also certified to 45,000 feet, which it could readily reach under a wide range of conditions.

Fuel capacity was not increased on the Citation V, so in spite of the more powerful engines, its IFR range is 1,960 nautical miles, a modest decrease from the S/II's 2,090 nautical miles reach.

One change from the S/II's wings and horizontal stabilizer was the de-icing system. The TKS weeping wing system was replaced with old-fashioned boots, but they were new, low-profile rubber from BF Goodrich. According to Cessna, there was no appreciable difference in the wing's

Chapter Three

Mid-sized Move

When Cessna announced three new Citations at the 1976 NBAA convention in Denver, Colorado, by far the most ambitious model was the Citation III. It was to be a brand new design that would take the Citation line into the ranks of mid-sized business jets. It would also be Cessna's most complex project to date that would push the company's design, manufacturing, and engineering resources to the limit.

The Citation VI is a refinement of the III, Cessna's first swept-wing midsized jet that could climb to 51,000 feet in the final stages of a mission at a light loading as fuel burned off. More important than its absolute ceiling was its ability to climb directly to 41,000 feet to avoid most airline traffic, enabling it to benefit from direct routings to further cut travel time.

Citation III by opting for an efficient T-tail configuration for the empennage.

The supercritical wings can claim the lion's share of the credit for giving the Citation III cruise speeds as high as 470 knots and a maximum operating speed of Mach .85, values that are beyond the capabilities of its contemporaries using the same engine.

The swept, supercritical wing required a roll control and lift dump system more complex than the ones found on previous Citations. In addition to its hydraulically boosted ailerons, the Citation III also has hydraulically actuated spoilers, four on each wing. One spoiler on each side provides roll augmentation for the corresponding aileron, two function as in-flight speed brakes, and all four are deployed as ground spoilers after touchdown. The spoilers can also all be deployed for an emergency descent in excess of 10,000 feet per minute.

The Citation III is certified to 51,000 feet and is equipped with an unusual feature to facilitate its descent in case of an explosive decompression. If the cabin blows, the autopilot initiates the descent, easing the jet into a 25 bank, and maintaining Vmo (maximum operating limit) all the way down to 14,000 feet. The system can automatically bring the Citation III down from 51,000 feet to 14,000 feet in only 3 minutes.

While the flight controls are hydraulically boosted, manual handling is so good that no backup is required for the hydraulic system. A rudder bias system compensates automatically for the yaw effect in case of an engine failure. Slow speed flying and short field performance are aided by electrically operated flaps.

To power the Citation III, Cessna broke with its Pratt & Whitney traditions by choosing Garrett TFE 731-3Bs, which provided 3,650 pounds of thrust each, more than any engine suitable for business jets that Pratt & Whitney was making at the time. The TFE 731 was developed by Garrett from an APU the company made and became a highly popular engine series for business jets, powering such airplanes as the Learjet 35 and 55, the Hawker 700, the Falcon 20, 50, and 900, and the IAI Astra, among others.

Aesthetes have complained about the III's blunt nose, but it is bulbous for a good reason. The svelte patrician nose with which it started flight testing proved to be an excellent ice accumulator, so it got a nose job that gave it its practical, ice-resistant plebeian proboscis.

The Citation III made its maiden flight on May 30, 1979. It went well, and the flight test and certification program was proceeding smoothly on schedule when it was dealt a setback by events beyond its control. In an aggressive reaction to a commercial

The Citation VI on final approach. Note the complex flaps and the absence of leading-edge slats. The flaps alone slow down the airplane's approach speeds sufficiently to give it greater flexibility when choosing airports with short runways.

A fine portrait of the Citation VI. It was designed to be an economic alternative to the VII, featuring an analog autopilot and a plain standard interior. But buyers of new jets wanted luxury and were willing to pay for it so only 39 were built.

airline crash that occurred five days before the III's first flight, the Federal Aviation Administration (FAA) changed the certification rules for aircraft certified under FAR 25 and insisted that the Citation III be modified to comply with the new requirements in mid-program.

The accident that caused the problem was the crash of a DC-10 departing from Chicago O'Hare. Shortly after rotation its left engine fell off and the airplane rolled over on its back into the ground. It was subsequently found that instead of removing the engine assembly from the wing in two sections as called for by the maintenance procedures, the airline's mechanics were saving time by easing the entire structure onto a forklift without separating the sections. This unorthodox procedure had weakened critical components of the support structure, which gave way at the worst possible moment.

The engine's separation failed critical control and hydraulic linkages, which played a part in downing the airplane. Taking the not entirely illogical view that the dire consequences of a catastrophic engine failure must be better guarded against, regardless of the failure's cause, the FAA rewrote chunks of the certification regulations, adding new requirements that primarily affected fuel supply protection, hydraulic and control line separation, and systems redundancy.

Having to comply with the new regulations set back the Citation III's certification schedule by a 1 1/2 years, added weight to the airplane— and worst of all— forced it to give up 900 pounds of fuel destined for its aft fuselage tank, which had to be scaled down to make way for some of the mods. The fuel loss amounted to 11 percent of the airplane's intended fuel load, and in a business where every extra pound

43

The Citation VII is a highly successful refinement of the Citation III, featuring more powerful engines and an advanced, first-generation glass cockpit. It also offered an interior that was entirely custom designed to suit the tastes of each owner. Only the highest standards of luxury were worthy of the acting flagship of the Citation fleet.

can be critical, it meant that the Citation III would just fall short of being a nonstop transcontinental business jet.

Cessna gained some measure of consolation in the knowledge that even with a fuel stop the III could beat some business jets coast to coast and that the majority of trips in business jets are much shorter anyway. Nevertheless, it was frustrating not to be able to deliver the performance promised because of external events.

Equally frustrating was the recession that had set in by the time the Citation III was certified in mid-1982. However, even with some order cancellations Cessna had over 100 firm orders in hand. The first delivery went to golf pro Arnold Palmer, who, as a pilot's pilot as well as a spokesman for the company, talked proudly of the abilities of his new "III Iron."

What Palmer and his fellow Citation III owners got was the fastest mid-sized business jet that had a 2,090-nautical mile IFR range and could escape the heavy airline traffic by being able to climb directly to 43,000 feet at maximum take-off weight. It also had plenty of passenger and baggage capacity even with a full fuel load, especially after a gross weight increase approved shortly after it was put in service.

The Citation III joined the Cessna family in a time of economic turmoil, caused not only by the general recession but also the dire condition of the piston engined market in which Cessna was the pre-eminent player. The whole piston-engined airplane industry collapsed, in large part because of the punishing stranglehold of America's aviation product liability laws. In 1980 Cessna realized sales of $1 billion for the first time, but by the mid-1980s it had shut down all single-engined production and its

The Citation VII was an early favorite of Executive Jet's NetJets fractional ownership program.

Chapter Four

CitationJet

A company rarely gets a chance to accomplish the same marketing coup twice, but Cessna did just that when it introduced the CitationJet two decades after the original Citation 500.

The CitationJet was the first of the very light jets, beating any competitors to the market by a decade. It can fly faster and farther on less thrust and fuel than the Citation 500.

This Paul Bowen shot of a CitationJet shows what many pilots love most about flying. Few environments are as seductive.

The CitationJet rolls out in 1991 to repeat the original Citation 500's success as an alternative to the turboprops. On less thrust than the 500, it delivered more speed while burning less fuel, demonstrating how far aerodynamics and engine technology had progressed in only two decades.

As mentioned earlier, by the early 1980s Pratt & Whitney Canada had significantly ratcheted up the price of its JT15D-1 engine that powered the Citation I, the entry-level direct competitor of the turboprops that embodied the original Citation ideal. The JT15D-1s were now going for barely less than the more powerful version powering the Citation II. Since the engines account for more than 30 percent of a jet's total cost, the price differential between the Citation I and II shrank to the point where it made little sense for customers to opt for the smaller jet. In 1985 Cessna reluctantly stopped production of the Citation I.

But at the same time, the company recognized that with the Citation I's demise the unfilled market niche that it had so brilliantly exploited with the original Citation 500 was about to re-emerge. There

was no competitively priced turbofan airplane to take on the turboprops.

Here was an opportunity to repeat history. If Cessna could once again create a 4-5 passenger turbofan airplane that delivered the requisite performance and operating economics at a price competitive with the turboprops, the company could capture the same lucrative market niche for the second time. And based on its Citation experience, Cessna had every reason to believe that it could do the job with a perky new entrant, the CitationJet.

The CitationJet's specs could have been photocopied from the original Citation proposal. The CitationJet would be a straight-winged entry-level jet as easy to fly as high-end piston twins and twin turboprops. It would be considerably faster than the

The CitationJet's original cockpit was one of the first light jets to feature EFIS equipment. It was upgraded to a third-generation glass cockpit on the CJ1 in 1998.

turboprops, yet its price and operating economics would be competitive with them. It would be approved for single-pilot operation, and would appeal particularly to entrepreneurial owner pilots.

There were additional challenges. As business jets had become increasingly popular, their passengers had grown accustomed to their high speed. Cessna itself had been successfully pushing up the speeds of the straight-winged Citations and had introduced its own super swift swept-wing line. A next generation "Slowtation" would no longer do. The new jet would have to be considerably faster than the original Citation 500, yet to keep its price competitive, it would have to achieve this goal on a less expensive engine providing less thrust.

Customer expectations had also become more sophisticated about cabin comfort. Passengers were

no longer inclined to deal with steps in the aisle where the wing spar played through the fuselage. The new jet would have to have a flat center aisle in its cabin all the way through.

Meeting such a tall order called for a command performance in aerodynamic design, and the design team's best efforts would come to nothing if a suitable engine failed to materialize. Cessna's engineers were up to the task and fortunately for them and the business jet world, the right engine did come along at the right time once again, just as the Pratt & Whitney JT15D had materialized in time for the Citation 500. It was the Williams Rolls FJ44, built by a company hitherto known for the engines it made to propel cruise missiles to their fiery end.

Cessna was well positioned to rise to the aerodynamic challenge. By the mid-1980s the company

A good view of the CitationJet's super-smooth natural laminar flow wing that is a key component of its commercial success. This wing retains laminar flow over 30 percent of its surface compared to a negligible percentage on the non-laminar flow wing.

had developed considerable in-house expertise in aerodynamics, paradoxically because the straight-winged Citations were slower than their contemporaries. To keep their airplane competitive without changing the straight-wing configuration, the company's engineers had become masters of the aerodynamic tweak. With the new S/II wing they broke the 400-knot barrier, and further refinement pushed the V, the largest straight-winged Citation, up to 430 knots in cruise, speeding it to within 30 knots of its swept-wing competitors. But most of the incremental gains in aerodynamics had been augmented by incremental increases in power to bump up the airplane's speed.

The new jet, however, would have less power than any Citation before it. Making it go faster than the original 500 would require more than incremental tweaking. The only solution that had the potential to yield the required results was the natural laminar flow wing. Such a wing retains unseparated, super-low drag laminar flow over a much larger section of the wing surface than traditional wings. It is a conceptually seductive objective, but one that is notoriously difficult to achieve while retaining good handling characteristics and maintaining ease of production.

Cessna's aeronautical engineers, however, were already ahead of the game. They had built a solid foundation of research experience with laminar flow design. In a joint research program with NASA spanning four years, they had installed an experimental laminar flow wing on a high-performance piston-powered single-engined Cessna 210 with promising results. Due to the efficiency achieved by the laminar flow wing, the experimental 210 had realized a 15 percent overall reduction in drag without any other changes to the airplane.

The CitationJet would be the first to benefit from the research project's promising results. The airframe design team set to work, and when it was finished had a wing that retained laminar flow for up to 31 percent of its surface from the leading-edge aft (a conventional wing barely retains laminar flow beyond the leading edge). This achievement was not only an admirable feat of theoretical design, but also a triumph of production engineering. To be able to meet on the assembly line the laminar flow

Next Page
The CitationJet retains the Citations' outstanding short field performance.

Comfortable club seating makes the CitationJet the ultimate 4- or 5-seater. The seats move away from the sidewall and pivot to provide relaxing unconstrained seating.

wing's exacting demands for contour precision and smoothness was as much of an achievement as getting the theory right.

To provide the super-smooth and sufficiently rigid wing surface required by the laminar flow wing, Cessna used slightly thicker wing skins than on other airplanes and had them chemically milled from a solid block of metal to provide additional rigidity. Weight was kept in check by using bonding exten-

To save weight and because it has great short field performance, the CitationJet features thrust attenuators instead of reversers. The paddles deploy outward to neutralize the flow out of the engines after landing.

sively to hold the wing together. Flush rivets were used only aft of the laminar flow area and they were exquisitely filled in, eliminating all traces of them.

Among the challenges of implementing the laminar flow wing was what to do about de-icing. De-icing boots were out of the question because they would disrupt laminar flow. The TKS weeping wing system employed on the S/II wing was not ideal because of the dense de-icing liquid's weight and sporadic uncertainties about its availability at FBOs. Electrically heating the entire leading edge was impractical.

The only other option was using engine bleed air, which raised questions of its own, given the Williams Rolls engines' comparatively low thrust. Any airflow diverted from the engine eats into its performance. Nevertheless, this option was Cessna's choice, and it proved to be a good one. The bleed air diverted is so hot that a small flow mixed with ambient air is enough for the job with a negligible reduction in engine performance.

There are other aerodynamic features that reduce drag. The empennage is in a T-tail configuration. Placing the horizontal stabilizer in the smoother air above the airflow coming off the slipstream makes it more efficient and allows it to be smaller and lighter.

A complex fuselage-wing fairing further reduces drag. It covers the spar carry through structure that runs under the fuselage to give the CitationJet a flat aisle throughout the length of its cabin. The fairing extends some distance both forward and aft of the wing center section and its curvature changes constantly. A lot of wind tunnel work and computer analysis went into its design that wasn't readily available to light jet designers back when the Citation 500 was created.

Lastly, the CitationJet also gains an aerodynamic benefit from the small frontal profile and light weight of its Williams Rolls engines, and the fact that they stand well away from the fuselage.

The Williams Rolls FJ 44-1A engines are as significant a technological advance as the laminar flow wing, and to them the CitationJet and a whole new class of very light jets owes its existence. They are lighter and more fuel efficient than any other

The Williams Rolls family of turbofans. They made the very light jet possible. The FJ 44-1A, which was launched by the CitationJet, has 700 moving parts compared to 2,500 on earlier generation turbofans.

turbofan in executive jet use, made possible by cutting-edge materials and production technology.

The FJ 44-1A engines have only about 700 moving parts compared to about 2,500 parts on the Pratt & Whitney JT15D-1s, and at 450 pounds per engine, they weigh 132 pounds less than the Pratt & Whitneys. They have the same bypass ratio, but are smaller in frontal section, run cooler, and burn 20 percent less fuel. While they produce 300 pounds less thrust, they have a higher thrust-to-weight ratio, and are less expensive.

This potent package is the creation of Dr. Sam Williams of Williams International, the company that made its name designing and building engines for cruise missiles, such as the Tomahawk. It is rumored from time to time that the CitationJet's engines are modified cruise missile engines, but this is not true.

Turbines designed to lie in storage for years and then work perfectly for a one-way trip to hell aren't directly transferable into day-in day-out-civilian jet use for thousands of hours before an overhaul. However, some of the techniques to build them are applicable and it was this know-how that Williams International relied on when it decided to get into making commercial jet engines to diversify away from its core business as the Cold War wound down.

The company started development of the engine for potential use in a new military jet trainer for the U.S. Air Force before deciding to bring it to the civilian market. Recognizing its lack of experience in the commercial jet engine business, Williams then teamed up with Rolls Royce to jointly complete development of the engine and to benefit from Rolls Royce's comprehensive global marketing and product support network. Williams was the lead manager of the engine program and Rolls Royce provided key hot section components.

One of the most notable parts of the FJ 44-1A engine is its fan disk, featuring Williams' own wide-sweep-fan technology that is key to delivering the engine's thrust and low fuel consumption. It is machined from a single chunk of titanium, blades and all. In more conventional engines, such as the JT15D series, each blade is a separate component. Remarkably, the entire Williams Rolls fan can be replaced for the same cost as replacing three blades on the JT15Ds, and damage can also be repaired by welding a piece of titanium onto the disk and machining it.

In order to save weight, the CitationJet's Williams Rolls engines were not equipped with thrust reversers. Instead, they have thrust attenuators, pioneered by Cessna on its T-37 Tweety Bird Air Force trainers. They are paddle-like panels that swing outward at a shallow angle, deflecting thrust sideways after touchdown to reduce its forward component. The flaps can also be extended to a 60-degree ground-only setting to further slow the ground roll.

The CitationJet's airframe-engine combination handsomely delivered the desired results. When the flight tests and certification were complete, Cessna had a new entry-level jet that far surpassed the original Citation 500. With a typical cruise speed of 380 knots it was 40 knots faster, it could fly 13 percent farther on 17 percent less fuel, and with a 45,000 feet ceiling it could fly 10,000 feet higher. It could routinely operate from runways shorter than 3,000 feet. And it costs less than the entry-level Citation I it replaced in Cessna's line up.

When Cessna introduced the CitationJet at the 1989 National Business Aviation Association convention, the response was overwhelming. The business jet

Chapter five

Mach .92

At the 1990 NBAA convention, Cessna created the show's biggest buzz by announcing that it would build the world's fastest business jet, the Mach .90-plus Citation X. The airplane would be a brand new, "clean sheet" design rather than a derivative.

An excellent portrait of the Citation X's belly fairing that is as important aerodynamically for keeping critical Mach in check as is the supercritical wing.

Its specifications placed the 8-10 passenger Citation X at the upper end of the mid-sized range of business jets, yet its performance projections put it more in league with larger jets while promising to retain the Citation line's renowned benign handling characteristics and short field capabilities. Its estimated $17 million price tag was somewhere in between the typical prices of the two groups of aircraft.

With the Citation X, Cessna was once again seeking to fill a niche others had ignored. The company's industry surveys had revealed that the concept of the executive jet as time machine had taken stronger hold than ever in the business aviation community. Corporations had to ever more closely justify any investment, and in the case of the corporate airplane, the measure was saving executive time

The Mach .92 Citation X is the fastest business jet in the world. More remarkably, it achieves its high speed at operating economies equivalent to much slower jets.

It may be the fastest, but the Citation X also has outstanding short field performance, thanks to a complex wing equipped with leading edge slats as well as three-section trailing-edge flaps.

The cross section of the Citation X engines together almost equal the cross section of the cabin. No wonder they pump out enough thrust to attain Mach .92.

at the lowest possible cost to boost productivity. In Cessna's judgement there was a sufficiently large group within the business jet community that valued the performance of the large jets but wasn't inclined to spend the money they commanded.

Business aviation's skeptic observers had other views, especially in the aftermath of the 1987 stock market crash. They spun out a laundry list of reasons why the Citation X had only a limited chance of success.

It would be too expensive for what it would deliver, they said. Its ambitious speed targets necessitated a frontal area that would make the cabin too cramped and narrow for such an expensive jet. Its speed advantage would make a difference only on long trips—a minority of business flights—which wouldn't be enough to justify its price. Buyers would prefer the slight additional expense for an airplane

This T-38 chase plane is ideal for keeping up with the prototype Citation X. At normal cruise, they are equal in speed.

The Citation X's cockpit is a pilot's dream. It is the first Citation to feature an EICAS screen (center) that displays all engine and systems information electronically on a need-to-know basis.

with a larger cabin. Its operating costs would be too high. The project was technically too ambitious to make good business sense, and so on and so on.

But the company that made millions by realizing there was a vast market for a jet slower than any other business jet drew an equally savvy conclusion about the market's high end. Speed sells!

Furthermore, Cessna was convinced that by applying cutting-edge aerodynamics and engine technology, it could make the Citation X attain the promised speed performance at operating expenses equal to the cost of flying mid-sized business jets that were approximately 10-15 percent slower in cruise. For the X to be a business success, this was the crucial performance target to meet.

Cessna politely put up with the doubters and quietly created a transonic work of art. When the Citation X was completed it could do everything Cessna had promised, and more. Its miserly operating costs were right on target and in high cruise it could routinely streak across the world at Mach .92.

Its design team was awarded the 1996 Collier Trophy for creating the first U.S. civilian aircraft capable of cruising at Mach .92, and it also caught the imagination of its target market. Arnold Palmer got the first Citation X, and it became the favorite of a new youthful breed of entrepreneurs who had made their millions while the X was being developed and who were ready to cash in some of their gains

Next Page
N1AP. Golf pro Arnold Palmer received the first Citation. A 16,000-hour pilot, he has owned and flown Citations from the beginning, starting with the straight-winged models.

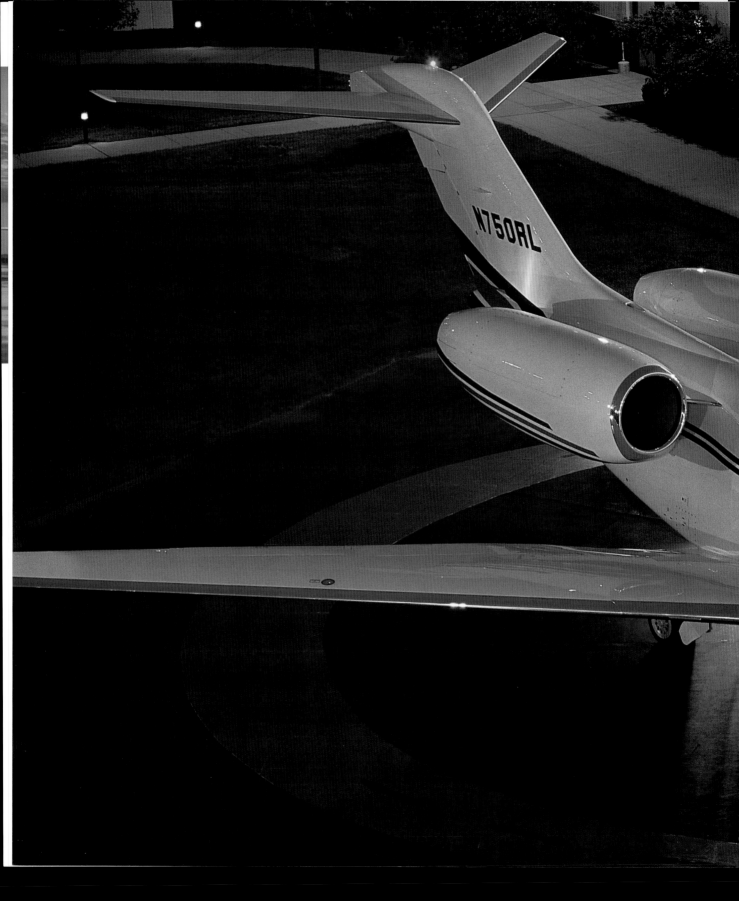

The 2,500^th Citation to be sold was a Citation X. Note the horseshoe emblem devised by ace marketeer Jim Taylor three decades before.

certified maximum ceiling of 51,000 feet. At optimal flight levels, it can cruise at its maximum Mach-operating limit of .92 and is a 500-plus knot airplane under most cruise conditions.

Its typical range with IFR reserves is approximately 3,300 nautical miles. That translates into nonstop reach between any two points in the United States and one-stop trips from California to Europe—at the fastest speeds in the class. With a little cooperation from the jet stream, the Citation X can cut west to east crossings of the United States to under four hours, and makes possible same-day coast-to-coast round trips in either direction with sufficient time to do business at the destination. In an early illustration of its high-speed global reach, a Citation X on a demo tour flew nonstop from Gander, Canada, to Casablanca, Morocco, in North Africa in only four hours.

For most companies that fly the Citation X, its speed advantage is measured by how it translates into increased productivity. For an Oklahoma-based oil services firm whisking its CEO between Tulsa and Washington on a regular basis, the Citation X saves him 50 hours a year that he would otherwise have to spend on airplanes. Similar time savings for other executives in the company add up to make the expense of the Citation X eminently worthwhile. Another CEO of a Midwestern Fortune 500 company started using a Citation X when his Gulfstream was down for maintenance. He so valued the 40 minutes the Citation saved him on a trip to the West Coast that it is now his preferred airplane.

The airplane's performance doesn't come at the cost of a good payload even at high fuel loads. Fully fueled, the X has room for 1,200 pounds, comfortably allowing six passengers and their baggage to fly the X to its limits.

While a bit on the narrow side for its price, the Citation X's passenger cabin is as luxurious as any

A Citation X taxis in after a trans-Atlantic flight. The X will comfortably cross the Atlantic non-stop in both directions in all weather.

Chapter Six

Citations for All

Cessna was well positioned to build on its lead in the light and medium business jet market as the 1990s got under way. The straight-winged Citation line was thriving and the mid-sized line was holding its own. Two brand new designs covered in the previous chapters, the CitationJet and the Citation X, were under development to significantly broaden the Citation's market reach.

The Bravo continues to draw the light jet crowd in the market for a best all-arounder. While it features avionics, engine, and system improvements over the Citation II, it is fundamentally similar to its illustrious predecessor, demonstrating the excellence of the original design.

The Bravo's avionics package is a far cry from the Citation II's analog mechanical gauges, but the engine instruments are little changed. The third-generation glass cockpit avionics package is one of the features the Bravo pilots like best.

The Bravo's interior has also benefited from progress in interior design since the first Citation IIs appeared.

The company also acquired an energetic new corporate parent. In 1992 General Dynamics--the concern that had helped Cessna through the challenging 1980s--sold the company to Textron, a diversified multinational conglomerate whose aviation interests also include Lycoming.

With its commitment to continuously expand and update its product line, coupled with advances in engine development and advances in avionics, Cessna had also built up great potential for developing a wide range of additional aircraft under the right market conditions.

And the conditions were soon to be right, for the 1990s proved to be a time of unprecedented economic boom in the United States, triggering an unparalleled level of demand for executive jets. In addition to massive corporate and individual wealth accumulation, two key factors played a role in steering the swelling ranks of the well to do into the business jet market: the steep deterioration of airline service and a corresponding growth in affordable fractional ownership opportunities in executive jets.

A Bravo in the foreground, flanked by a III to the right and a X to the left. The three airplanes represent three decades of Citation evolution reaching all the way back to the Citation II.

To maximize profits in their world of cutthroat competition, the airlines were becoming masters of what they call "yield management" at the expense of business travelers. They increasingly charged wildly differing prices for the same class of seat on the same flight, depending on shifting daily demand for tickets on the route. Business travelers who had little flexibility to make advanced purchases and select advantageous travel dates were routinely having to pay usurious prices compared to leisure travelers.

It was not uncommon for a business person on a nonstop same-day mid-week return flight from Boston to St. Louis traveling in economy class to pay $1,600 for a ticket while the tourist sitting next to him paid only $160 for his return trip because he was able to stay over on Saturday in St. Louis before flying home. By comparison, the typical hourly charter rate for a Citation II was less than $1,600, so it didn't take too many company executives traveling together to make jet charter an attractive alternative. The hourly operating costs of the same jet were even lower. An increasing number of firms and individuals in the position to invest capital in a jet were finding that it made good business sense to do so.

Another deterioration in airline service that played a role in popularizing business jets was the decreasing number of destinations served by direct flights, forcing travelers to connect through hubs notorious for lengthy delays and flight cancellations. When the days of lost productivity were factored in due to missed connections and cancelled airline flights, the case for the executive jet alternative on such trips was further reinforced.

The other development that gave the executive jet industry a massive boost was the rapid growth of fractional ownership. The concept was pioneered by Richard Santulli of Executive Jet, who started his NetJets program with a fleet of Citation S/IIs.

A fractional program offers shares as little as one-eighth in a business jet which is one of a large fleet of identical jets owned by a pool of fractional owners and operated by a program manager. An owner's one-eighth share provides 100 occupied hours per year in the fleet's jets and guarantees availability on short notice. Owners who need no more than 100 hours per year can spend $1 million on an $8 million jet and get exactly the same benefits out of it as if they had bought the whole airplane.

Next Page
The Citation Excel combines the X's fuselage with the Ultra's wing to create the only light jet with a stand-up cabin.

The comforts of the Excel's stand-up cabin surpass other light jets. Being the only light jet with a stand-up cabin made the Excel an instant best seller.

Fractional ownership opened a vast new market for executive jets. As many as 80 percent of customers who bought fractional shares had never owned a business airplane before. Executive Jet, which dominates the field to this day, expanded so aggressively that by 1995 to 1997 it accounted for $3.5 billion in aircraft orders, amounting to half the global new business jet sales for the period. Prominent among Executive Jet's orders were various models of Citations.

With the increased demand for business jets came a preference for a greater range of models tailored to specific needs that would provide a wider choice among light, medium, and heavy jets and blur the distinction between the categories.

Cessna enthusiastically seized these opportunities. By the second half of the 1990s the company was putting into service the Citation Bravo, successor to the Citation II, and the Excel, the only light jet with a stand-up cabin. Also on the way were the CJ1 and the

The Excel on a test flight. The blue components are composite. The test flight results were used to fine tune the Excel to deliver its promised performance.

The Excel's cockpit is similar to that of the Ultra. Standardization of the sophisticated glass cockpits is a hallmark of the latest-generation Citations.

CJ2, successors to the CitationJet, the Ultra Encore, an upgrade of the Citation Ultra, and a new transcontinental mid-sized jet, the Citation Sovereign.

The Bravo is nothing more than the latest incarnation of the venerable Citation II, the jet first launched in 1976, produced until 1985, and brought back by popular demand in 1989. Announced in 1994 and put in service in 1997, the Bravo features major improvements over the II without compromising its impeccable manners and low-key operating costs that made it Cessna's best selling jet of all time.

The Bravo's most significant new feature is its new-generation Pratt & Whitney 500-series engine, the PW530A. Its 2,750 pounds of thrust brings a 10 percent improvement over the power put out by the trusty old JT15D-4s, and more importantly, its fuel specifics are better by 15 percent. More power on less fuel adds up to impressive results. The 14,800-pound Bravo is a 403-knot airplane in normal cruise with the original Citation II wings. Its climb performance is also improved over the Citation II and its IFR range is extended to 1,600 nautical miles, carrying six passengers and a crew of two.

Another big improvement implemented on the Bravo is one that is perhaps even more welcomed by its pilots than the power upgrade. The Citation II's successor is equipped at last with forgiving trailing link landing gear that takes all the bounce out of touchdowns, unlike the stiff straight-legged main gear of earlier models that required pilots to cross their fingers and hope for the best for a smooth arrival no matter how well they flew the airplane.

The Excel's massive trailing-link landing gear takes the bump out of arrivals. Today the entire Citation line features trailing-link gears, a big improvement over the earlier models' straight struts that were prone to firm arrivals.

The Bravo's cockpit also benefited from a major upgrade, getting a highly integrated third-generation avionics suite. Its Honeywell Primus 1000 flight guidance system features two Primary Flight Displays and one Multifunction Display. Allied Signal radios and a GNS-X long-range navigation system completes the package.

Cessna markets the Citation Bravo heavily as an alternative to the Raytheon King Air B200 turboprop. The company is so confident in the Bravo's low operating costs that it formally guarantees them to be lower per hour than a King Air 200's.

While the Bravo was well received, the airplane that generated the most buzz among the light jets was the Citation Excel, which Cessna pitched as the mid-sized jet for a light jet price. One long-standing complaint about light jets is that they lack a stand-up cabin, and with the Excel, Cessna decided to do something about that.

The Excel was an ingenious move by Cessna to combine components of a straight-wing and a swept-wing Citation to create a third airplane that hit a home run out of its own ballpark. The Excel is basically an Ultra wing and empennage mated to a Citation X fuselage to create a stand-up cabin light jet, albeit one that comes close to the mid-sized league with its 20,200-pound maximum take-off weight.

Creating the Excel was, of course, a much more complex exercise than just slapping together the different airframe components and going flying. A lot of original aerodynamic and structural design work had to be done to successfully bring off the fusion.

The Ultra wing's span was extended by 3.5 feet and major redesign had to be done on the center section to mate it with the fuselage in a manner that keeps it from passing through the passenger cabin and creating a step in the aisle. The cabin floor is unobstructed for its entire length, a feature that has become the norm among modern business jets.

The wing's surface was also tweaked to handle the new hybrid airframe's aerodynamic characteristics. A modest stall fence on each wing, vortex generators, and boundary layer energizers along the leading edge outward of the stall fences manage the airflow to ensure continued impeccable handling near the stall.

The fuselage-wing joint is faired in with an elongated belly fairing that keeps the airflow acceleration and deceleration around the fuselage as gradual as

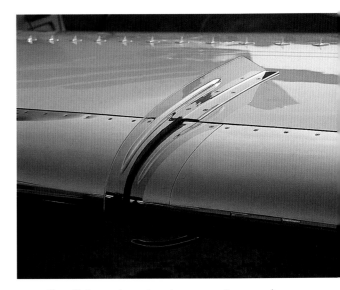

A small stall fence, boundary layer energizers, and vortilons manage low-speed airflow on the Excel's wing.

The CJ1 features an all-new glass cockpit. Integrated primary flight displays and mulifunction displays have replaced the dozens of analog gauges of an earlier generation.

possible to minimize drag. For benign stall recovery there are two delta fins under the tail which are set at an angle to help pitch the nose down as the airplane approaches the stall. They are similar to the fins that first appeared on the Learjet 55C.

The horizontal stabilizer is also slightly modified from the one found on the Ultra. Because the Excel is bigger and heavier than the Ultra, its elevator forces are also heavier under certain flight regimes. The option of increasing the horizontal stabilizer's size to lighten the loads would have added weight, which Cessna wanted to avoid. The

designers decided instead to keep the stabilizer the same size, but make its position adjustable by linking it to the flaps. To keep stick forces in the pleasant range throughout the envelope, the horizontal stabilizer moves automatically with changes in flap settings, adjusting its angle of incidence to the appropriate position for each phase of flight.

At the Citation Excel's heart is its pair of powerful Pratt & Whitney PW545A engines which are thermodynamically rated at 4,200 pounds of thrust each, but are flat rated on the airplane to 3,803 pounds, leaving room for growth. They are

The CJ2 is a stretched CJ1 with more powerful engines. This development of the model is reminiscent of the Citation I–II story. With more even more powerful, fuel-efficient Williams-Rolls engines coming on stream it is legitimate to wonder how far the basic CitationJet design will evolve.

The CJ2's cockpit is identical to the CJ1's, making it easier for pilots who are transitioning into the new jet.

Two extra seats expand the CJ2's cabin load. The CJ2 is also faster by 20 knots and can fly 200 nautical miles further.

The Encore is a souped-up Ultra.

Pratt & Whitney's latest generation engines, with twice the bypass ratio of the JT15D-5As that power the Ultra and with a 15 percent improvement in specific fuel consumption.

The engines come with a simple form of electric engine control that can automatically set takeoff, climb, and cruise power but also retains the full mechanical linkages to the engine which can be selected at the pilot's discretion. The Excel thus has the best of both worlds and may be dispatched with the electric engine controls inoperative.

The engines have sufficient power to provide bleed air for de-icing the wing without any power penalty. This allows the Excel to dispense with the Ultra's de-icing boots.

The Excel's cockpit is standard Citation Ultra and its passenger cabin comfort and elegance is pure Citation X. The cabin also retains the X's pressure differential. This gives the Excel a cabin altitude of only 6,800 feet at its maximum certified altitude of 45,000 feet compared to the more typical 8,000 feet at a business jet's maximum cruising altitude.

The Excel's top cruise speed is 430 knots. It can climb straight to 41,000 feet at its 16,630-pound gross weight in just 20 minutes and 45,000 feet is also within reach shortly thereafter under most conditions. With four passengers and two crew members on board, its IFR range is a respectable 2,080 nautical miles, and it retains the straight-winged Citation line's good short field performance. Even at a mile-high airport on a 59-degree day, it needs only 4,840 feet for takeoff at gross weight. On arrival, its hefty trailing link landing gear softens the return to terra firma.

The Encore's panel has much in common with the rest of the contemporary straight-winged Citations.

The Citation Excel proved to be another great coup for Cessna as soon as it was launched, proving once again that the company is exceptionally perceptive about the market's desires. It registered well over 250 orders by the turn of the millennium with an order backlog stretching into 2002. One of the first customers for the Excel was Executive Jet, which audaciously ordered 50 Excels at once for its NetJets Fractional program long before the prototype's first flight.

Even though the entire Citation line was selling at an increasingly brisk pace by the mid-1990s, Cessna couldn't afford to rest on its laurels as other manufacturers were also racing to introduce new models to the buoyant market. Challengers emerged from several quarters to the CitationJet's monopoly in the very light business jet market, the strongest among them being Raytheon's Premiere I. In 1998 Cessna made a two-pronged move to protect the CitationJet's market position by announcing two derivatives of the little jet, the CJ1 and CJ2.

The CJ1 is an incremental upgrade of the CitationJet, incorporating the latest advances in avionics by equipping the airplane with an advanced two-tube Collins Pro Line 21 glass cockpit featuring 8X10 display screens. Even the engine information is displayed on the multifunction display instead of individual gauges, a first for a jet the CJ1's size. Another modification was a modest gross weight upgrade that slightly increased the CJ1's useful load.

The CJ2 is a more ambitious derivative of the CitationJet and a more direct attempt to pre-empt the competition. It also echoes Cessna's past experience, being eerily reminiscent of the original Citation 500's upgrade to the Citation II.

The CJ2 is basically a stretched CitationJet, re-engined with a more powerful version of the original Williams Rolls FJ44 engine. The fuselage is lengthened by almost three feet, increasing the CJ2's cabin seating to 6/7 from 4/5 on the CitationJet. To efficiently handle the upscaled airplane, the wing span is also increased by three feet.

The Williams FJ44-2C engines are a development of the FJ44-1A's, providing 2,300 pounds of thrust each, a hefty 400 pounds increase per side. This is the same engine being used on the Raytheon Premiere I and another sleek, ambitious challenger, the Sino Swearingen SJ30-2. Up front the CJ2's cockpit is identical to the CJ1's and in the straight-winged Citation tradition, both jets may be flown by a single pilot.

The performance figures reveal the CJ2 derivative's payoff. In addition to being able to carry two more passengers, its maximum cruise speed is 400 knots, up from 380 knots on the CJ1; its range with 45-minute reserves is 1,680 nautical miles, up from 1,475 nautical miles; its useful load is 4,898 pounds compared to 3,900 pounds; and its maximum take-off weight is 12,300 pounds compared to 10,600 pounds.

Similar to the relationship between the Citation I and II two decades before, the CJ1 and CJ2 are complementary airplanes, serving two close but distinctly different markets. As the Citation I and its replacement, the original CitationJet have shown, there continues to be an enduring demand for a light jet with a cabin for four.

Concurrent with developing more capable derivatives of the CitationJet, Cessna also found time to tweak the Citation Ultra into the Encore. As its name suggests, the Encore is a rewarding repeat performance of the best parts of the score played by the original Ultra. A new, more modern and powerful engine and a further refined wing are the main treats of the Ultra's encore.

Like the Bravo and the Excel, the Encore was equipped with an appropriate model of Pratt & Whitney's new 500-series engine, in this case the PW535A, which provides a 10 percent increase in thrust and a 16 percent improvement in specific fuel consumption over the Ultra's JT15D-5As.

As on the Excel, the new engine was powerful enough to provide bleed air for de-icing the wings without giving up any performance, enabling Cessna to do away with the rubber de-icing boots in favor of a smooth metal leading edge. As on the Excel, a small stall fence on each wing and a variety of vortex generators and boundary layer energizers keep the Encore well mannered approaching the stall.

The Encore made history in a minor way by being the last descendant of the original Citation 500 to be upgraded to trailing link main landing gear, making the stiff straight struts and their firm arrivals history. The bulkier trailing link gear reduced the space available in the wings for fuel by 516 pounds from 5,814 pounds to 5,298 pounds, but the Encore's superior specific fuel consumption manages to give it minutely better range than the Ultra (1,700 nautical miles vs. 1,660 nautical miles IFR). A 431-knots maximum cruise speed, increased climb performance, better short field capabilities, and better operating economics are Cessna's reward for turning the Ultra into the Encore.

Cessna's closing act for the 20th century was appropriately the bridge that took the company into the new millennium in Citation style. It was the Citation Sovereign, a new, super mid-sized transcontinental business jet that would neatly fit into the product line between the company's flagship Citation X and the VII.

Like its predecessors, the Sovereign is another sensible Citation, artfully blending range, speed,

The Sovereign's cabin is as comfortable as the one on the Citation X.

cabin, comfort, systems simplicity, ease of handling, outstanding short field performance, a competitive price, and operating economics to give the market exactly what it wants.

Like the Excel, the Sovereign borrows its fuselage from the Citation X, which is mated to a newly designed mildly swept natural laminar flow wing to achieve the desired performance with the power and payload specified for the airplane. Power comes from two FADEC-equipped Pratt & Whitney PW306C engines that provide 5,686 pounds of thrust per side.

The Sovereign is intended to be a true transcontinental workhorse with a 2,500-nautical mile NBAA IFR range carrying eight passengers at 400 knots. On shorter distances it can cruise at speeds up to 445 knots. Its maximum certified altitude is 47,000 feet.

The Sovereign's cockpit is equipped with a state-of-the-art Honeywell Primus Epic CDS avionics suite featuring four 8X10 display screens and the latest terrain and traffic avoidance systems.

The Sovereign's cabin is as comfortable as the one on the Citation X with good reason. It is fundamentally identical. While slower than Cessna's flagship Citation X, the Sovereign is also significantly less expensive. In value for investment its performance is hard to beat.

FRACTIONAL PIONEERS

Fractional ownership and NetJets were corporate and personal aviation's blockbuster success story of the 1990s in which Citations played a prominent role. The concept was invented by Richard Santulli, mathematics Ph.D., former Wall Street banker, CEO of Executive Jet, and founder of its NetJets program.

NetJets offers fractional shares in different fleets of identical aircraft. An aspiring jet setter can buy as little as one-eighth share in one aircraft in a fleet of identical jets for about an eighth of the jet's total price. That entitles him to the use of all the identical aircraft in that particular fleet for up to 100 hours per year. A fractional owner has the advantages of full ownership for a fraction of its price.

Availability is the usual problem in one or two shared airplanes because each owner wants to fly at the same time. But programs like NetJets are able to guarantee aircraft availability because they have large fleets of identical fractionally owned airplanes and the jets are fast, able to reach any point in the country in a matter of hours. When a call comes in for an airplane, NetJets dispatches the one most conveniently available.

Santulli's discovery that beyond a certain fleet size availability ceases to be a problem given the predictable nature of travel patterns was the breakthrough that made fractional ownership the success it has become. "It's a pure mathematical relationship," he likes to say.

Financial predictability, tax advantages, and operational advantages are other attractions of fractional ownership. At the end of the contract or at any time after the first two years, NetJets is obligated to buy back a share at fair market value. The management fee and hourly operating costs are contractually predetermined and indexed to inflation. A share makes available all the tax benefits of owning an airplane, such as depreciation.

Fractional owners need not worry about hangaring, hiring crews, managing operations, and maintenance. If an airplane scheduled to serve a fractional owner experiences a technical problem, it disappears and an identical one materializes in its place. Owners with a need for different types of airplanes may buy fractional shares in each of them. They may also exchange the time they have in their airplane type for time in a more or less capable type, paying the difference in the hourly operating costs.

When Santulli decided to take the plunge in 1986 after crunching the numbers, he chose six Citation S/IIs to kick off the program. Today the fleets managed by NetJets amount to hundreds of jets worth billions of dollars. Citations are prominent among them. Billionaire investor Warren Buffet liked the idea so much that in 1998 he bought the company for $750 million.

The market has such confidence in Cessna's ability to deliver on its promises that the company got 80 orders for the Sovereign worth $1.1 billion in the first two weeks when it began marketing the airplane before its formal announcement at the 1998 NBAA convention. Riding the booming fractional market that it created, Executive Jet ordered 50 Sovereigns worth $650 million with options on another 50, confident that it could find fractional buyers by the time the airplanes began arriving off the assembly line.

As the 20th century came to a close, the Citation's success had far exceeded its pragmatic creators' greatest expectations. Although the Citation 500 entered the business jet world to corner a specific niche, Cessna has always prided itself on serving a broad spectrum of general aviation. The 500's descendants have lived up handsomely to that corporate ethos.

With more than 3,000 Citations sold and holding well over half the global market for light- and medium-sized business jets, Cessna provides the widest range of choice from the coolest very light jet to the sexiest, fastest, fire-breathing rocket ship of a Citation X. If the first three decades of Citations are anything to go by, the 21st century will be a wild and wonderful ride.

Index